Piecing Back the PEACE:

LIFE AFTER DIVORCE

All rights reserved, including the right to
reproduce this book or portions thereof in
any form whatsoever. The scanning, uploading,
and electronic sharing of any part of
this book without the permission of the publisher
is unlawful piracy and theft of the
authors intellectual property. If you would like to
use this material from the book
(other than for review purposes) prior written
permission must be obtained by
contacting the author at:
info@drtammycannon.com.
Thank you for your support of the author's rights.

ISBN:979-8-9900899-1-4

Copyright © 2024 Dr. Tammy Cannon Williams
All rights reserved.

❖❖❖ Table of Contents ❖❖❖

Dedication

Preface

Section I: **Braving New Beginnings**

Chapter 1   Shattered Pieces..................14

Chapter 2   Embracing New Beginnings....17

Chapter 3   Cultivating Resilience............21

Section II: **Soulful Healing**

Chapter 4   Rediscovering Independence...26

Chapter 5   Rebuilding your Life............30

Chapter 6   Finding your Inner Strength...34

Chapter 7   Emotional Roller Coasters..........42

Section III: Courage to Blossom

Chapter 8　　　　Self-Care and Wellness 47

Chapter 9　　　　Celebrating your Triumphs....52

Chapter 10　　　Reconnecting with your Passions...58

Chapter 11　　　Healing Within................62

Section IV: Piecing Back the Peace

Chapter 12　　　Regaining Peace...............67

Chapter 13　　　Navigating Finances..........76

Chapter 14　　　A Leap of Faith................85

Chapter 15　　　Regaining Trust................91

Chapter 16　　　Paying it Forward..............95

Chapter 17　　　The End.........................99

Dedication

This book is dedicated to all my sisters in Christ who purposed in their hearts, minds, and souls to be the strong Christian wives God called them to be.

To my mother, Marie Cannon, whom I love with all my heart. To my sisters, Phyllis Daniels and Major Kim Wilson, and my daughter Tierra Barnes, who are excellent examples of wives after God's own heart. Thank you for your love, prayers, and support when I needed it most. Be blessed, I love you dearly, and God bless you always.

To my husband, Chief Richard R. Williams, United States Navy, who came into my life and became a huge part of my peace. He stepped in and cared for me and my three small children.

I thank him for his unwavering love, support, and vision for us as a family. Thank you, my one and only true love, for helping me put my "Peace" back together.

To my brother, Dr. James Cannon, and my son, Theo "Skeeter" Lindsey, and Terrance, thank you so much for always being my greatest supporters. Thank you for the guidance and the encouragement to be the best I can be.
To my bonus brother, my nephew Nick Cannon. Thank you for allowing me to work on this project and helping me reach this goal.

Preface

I studied my Bible and other books on how to be a great wife. For years, I prepared myself, and one day, I met the man I thought I would be with forever. I did everything I could to make my home a Christian environment. I supported my ex-husband in all areas of his life.

One day, he realized that he no longer wanted or needed to be married. My ex-husband, whom I cherished, told me that he was no longer in love with me. He explained how much he loved me, but he was not in love.

You would think that this devastated me, but when I say that God will give you the peace that passes all understanding, I mean just that. When my ex-husband spoke those words to me, I was hurt, and I was disappointed, but I had so much strength. In fact, I felt like a burden was lifted from me. My marriage was not always peaceful – not by far.

When my ex-husband started sharing how he felt, God gave me amazing strength and peace. He showed me that my ex-husband's strongholds were no longer mine. He let me see that He was releasing me and pulling me out of a worsening situation.

My sisters, be strong and put all your trust in the Lord. He will deliver you from a destructive husband and from a toxic relationship. May God bless you and keep you. If you are in a toxic, dysfunctional marriage, or relationship, go to the Lord and ask Him to help you, to lead you and to guide you.

If you have ever been through a dysfunctional, toxic marriage and God has delivered you, please share your testimony with other ladies and let them know that God has not forgotten them.

Psalm 34:17 says, "The righteous cry, and the Lord heareth, and delivereth them out of all their troubles." God will give you peace and strength. All praises be to our Lord and Savior Jesus Christ.

My Story

On November 12, 1994, I got married. Like most young brides, I was filled with love and excitement. I had lived with my parents up until the day that I got married.

The first few years were exciting, and I felt like we truly loved one another. I had always wanted to be a wife. My mother was an excellent wife, and I wanted to follow in her footsteps. I had just finished my associate degree and worked as a preschool teacher.

I was very excited about my new journey as a wife and looking forward to being a mother one day. He was also working. We spent a lot of time together and we began planning our future as husband and wife. We set goals to have children, purchase a home, and maybe one day I would return to college.

One night, my ex-husband did not come home, it was around 1:00 am. My first thought, like many wives in marriage, was to be angry, but after a few hours, the thoughts of anger turned into thoughts of concern.

I had been watching the news. On the news, I saw a man who looked just like my ex-husband, wearing the same color of clothing that I last saw my ex-husband wearing. The guy had been shot, and he was lying on the ground.

I called around to various hospitals, and I called my parents. My parents told me to come to their house if I could, or they would come and get me. I drove to my parents' home.

When I arrived, my mother told me to call the house one more time. I called my house, and my ex-husband answered. I immediately began to cry. I was relieved at that time, knowing that he was home safe, but I was puzzled about where he had been. Why had he not called?

This was just the beginning of my nights of staying up, waiting, and wondering where my ex-husband could be and when he would come home. At the time, I did not know what my husband was doing or what he was involved in. But I knew that whatever it was, it was bigger than me and that God would need to intervene.

In August 1996, we welcomed a baby boy into our family. One day, eight months later, my ex-husband looked worried; he constantly told me he loved me, but he did not look the same. I knew something was wrong. I told him to talk to me. I told to him that whatever he was going through, I would be there for him and that I would not be angry.

He finally told me that he had slept with another woman. He told me what had happened, and I was hurt and disappointed. We regrouped, we got involved in our church, I forgave him, and we continued with our marriage. We continued working on our marriage. I saw a positive change in my ex-husband, and three years later, we welcomed a baby girl.

In April 2001, I saw the same look and behavior from my ex-husband that I had seen previously. We were two weeks away from purchasing our first home. Once again, I told him that if he needed to share something with me, go ahead and share. I told him that I would not be angry with him. I really just wanted him to release everything. He asked me, "How do you tell your wife that you messed up again?"

We went to our pastor in hopes of working things out. The second time he cheated was not as hurtful as the first time. The disappointment was already there, so we continued in our marriage.

We continued to have many ups and downs in the marriage. He would gain and lose jobs at an alarming rate; we moved several times, and he just would not stay employed. I was preparing my exit plan, and then, in 2005, I became pregnant. In 2006, we welcomed our third and last child.

I was excited about the pregnancy, but the relationship was still on the rocks. But I am so thankful for my son; I realized why he was born. I could see that the relationship needed to end, but I still stayed married. I trusted God and I did not want two little boys to be in a household with a father, so I continued.

Fast forward to 2008. It seemed that we were ok in our marriage. My ex-husband had issues with employment and was missing in action. However, even going through trials and tribulations, God will put a shield of protection around you. Even when everything is falling apart, God will allow you to walk in grace. Those weapons that are formed against you will not prosper. God will continue to protect you and work everything out for your good.

I would talk to the Lord and say, "Lord, he is your child. You must deal with him and get him to turn from whatever was causing him to move out of his flesh."

When you turn everything over to the Lord, the joy comes. God gives us the peace that we need to carry on. God gives us the ability to speak peaceful words and sleep peaceful nights when we trust Him and not man.

As godly wives, we want to do what is right for our families and often go through things we do not understand. We take things that we shouldn't have to take. My sisters, God is always by your side. He sees the tears, and He hears the prayers.

Continue to pray. Forget about trying to change your husband into something that he may not be. Get yourself together, run to the Lord, and He will help you. He will deliver you from all your troubles. Galatians 6:17 tells us, "From henceforth let no man trouble me: for I bear in my body the marks of the Lord Jesus."

Go ahead, cry, and let it all out. After the tears, gain strength, be strong in the Lord, and do not let anything come between you and your relationship with Jesus Christ. God will wipe away the tears and give you joy. The joy of the Lord is your strength. Make it your mission to pursue the joy of the Lord.

Stop feeling sorry for yourself and the situation that you are in. You are an overcomer. You are more than a conqueror; you are a child of God. Ask God how you can help other women in a similar situation, regain your strength, and use this time to volunteer and share your testimony. Many women feel they are going through something no one else has gone through. Let these women know that they are not the first and they will not be the last to go through a toxic relationship. Help build them up and encourage them.

There may be times when you feel down and need some encouragement from those whom you have just encouraged. You might have nights of crying, and you might think that you cannot make it on your own. God is with you and will never leave or forsake you. God is always by your side and will carry you through this situation as He always has.

God loves you. He knows exactly what you need and what needs to happen in your life. Trust Him and strive to gain a stronger relationship with Him and watch and see how He shields you from anything negative that tries to destroy your mind and your life.

My sisters, in Psalm 30:5, the Word of God says, "…weeping may endure for a night, but joy cometh in the morning." Blessings to every who reads this book. Be inspired, gain strength and trust God.
With love,

Dr. Tammy Cannon Williams

Section I:

BRAVING NEW BEGINNINGS

"For this reason, a man will leave his father and mother and be united to his wife, and the two will become one flesh. So they are no longer two, but one flesh. Therefore what God has joined together, let no one separate."

(Mark 10:7–9, NIV)

CHAPTER ONE

SHATTERED PIECES

The finality of the words, "I do not love you anymore," echoed through the empty chambers of my heart, ricocheted off walls built by years of shared dreams and memories. As the door closed behind him, it wasn't just the end of my marriage; it felt like the end of my life. But, as I would come to learn in the journey that followed, it was not an end at all. It was a beginning, a painful yet profoundly transformative new chapter of my life.

Divorce, I discovered, is more than a legal dissolution of a marriage; it's a seismic shift in one's identity and reality. The life you planned is suddenly painted over with uncertainty and fear. Who am I without my partner? What does my future hold? Questions like these hovered like specters in the newly hollowed walls of existence. But within this very void, the space left behind, new possibilities begin to whisper.
In the aftermath, survival was my sole focus.

I moved through the days mechanically, attending to the necessities of life, my children, but little else. The world continued its relentless spin, indifferent to my inner upheaval. Family and friends offered well-intentioned advice, but the words often felt like missives from a foreign land.

The only truth that I clung to was that I needed to move through the pain, not around it. Slowly, as the days stretched into weeks and months, a subtle shift began. The acute pain doled into a chronic ache. In the spaces between grief and longing, moments of clarity began to emerge. I realized that while I couldn't control the end of my marriage, I could control my response to it. I could be the victim of my story, or I could be the hero. I chose the latter.

This book, dear reader, is about recognizing that every ending is laden with the seeds of new beginnings. It's about understanding that, while you can't go back and change the beginning, you're entirely in charge of where you go from here. You have the power to redefine your life, to rebuild it, to reflect on who you are now, not who you were when you shared it with someone else.

In the pages that follow, we will explore the stages of grief and healing, the importance of self-care and community, and the practical steps to reclaiming your independence and joy.

We will dive into rediscovering your passions, redefining your goals, and, ultimately, reconstructing a life that is authentically and unapologetically yours.

The journey will not be easy. There will be days when the weight of what you've lost seems unbearable. But remember, it is often in our deepest pain that we find our greatest strength. As you stand at this crossroads between your past and potential future, know you are not alone. I am here with you, having walked this path myself. Together, we will step boldly into the promise of what's to come.

The end of your marriage is not the end of your story. It's simply the end of a chapter. And as one chapter closes, another opens, ripe with the potential for joy, growth, and then imaginable beauty.

Welcome to your new beginning. Let's begin the journey together.

Affirmations of Peace

I take a leap of faith into the unknown, trusting in my ability to heal and transform. I am on a journey of soulful healing and self-discovery.

CHAPTER TWO

EMBRACING NEW BEGINNINGS

Divorce can be one of the most challenging and emotional experiences in a person's life. It's a time of uncertainty, headache, and significant change. In 2008, I turned to my nephew, Nick Cannon, and told him that I was getting a divorce. Nick looked at me and said, "New Beginnings."

I do not know what I expected him to say, but those words helped me realize that life was not over. I'm sure that Nick does not remember those words that he shared with me, but those words gave me a different mindset. Instead of feeling sorry for myself, I realized that I indeed could start over and create a new beginning. I realized that within this similarly seemingly daunting journey lies a glimmer of hope and the opportunity for new beginnings.

Embracing new beginnings means acknowledging that the end of a marriage is not the end of your story. It's the opening of a new chapter, an opportunity to redefine yourself, your goals, and your life. It's about turning a page and facing the blank canvas of your future with courage, optimism, and an open heart.

The first step in embracing new beginnings after divorce is to reframe your negative. Instead of seeing yourself as a victim of circumstances, view
this as a chance to become the author of your own story. You can shape your future, guided by your desires and values. Moving forward requires letting go of the past. This doesn't mean erasing the memories or dismissing the lessons learned from your marriage but rather releasing the emotional baggage holding you back.

It's essential to free yourself from resentment, guilt, and regrets, as they can hinder your ability to fully embrace the present and future. Divorce often forces you to rediscover who you indeed are beyond the roles you played in your marriage. Take this opportunity to reconnect with your authentic self. Reflect on your interests, passions, and dreams that may have taken a back seat during your marriage. What brings you joy and fulfillment? Who are you when you are not defined by the marital status? Reconnect with your inner essence, and let it guide you.

Change can be unsettling, but it is an integral part of life. Embrace it with open arms, for within change lies growth and transformation. Welcome the uncertainty as a chance to learn, adapt, and evolve. Your comfort zone may have been shaken, but this is where you can discover your resilience and capacity for personal growth.

New beginnings often come with new goals. What do you want to achieve in this next phase of your life? Set clear, achievable goals that align with your values and aspirations. These goals will give you direction and purpose, whether it's pursuing a new career, taking up a hobby, or nurturing deeper connections with loved ones.

Amidst the pain of divorce, it may be challenging to find things to be grateful for. However, cultivating gratitude can be a powerful tool for embracing new beginnings. Focus on the positives in your life – supportive friends, family, personal strengths, and the freedom to create the life you desire. Gratitude can help shift your perspective and bring positivity into your journey.

Embracing new beginnings doesn't mean you have to do it alone. Seek support from friends, family, or therapists who can provide guidance and a listening ear during this transition. Their encouragement and empathy can be invaluable as you navigate this unchartered territory.

Embracing new beginnings after divorce is a linear process, a journey field with ups and downs. It's about finding the strength to pick yourself up when you stumble, staying true to your values, and believing in the possibilities that lie ahead.

In the face of adversity, remember that you have the resilience to not only survive but to thrive. Embrace this new chapter with courage and optimism, for within it, you have the chance to create a life that truly reflects your desires and dreams.

Affirmations of Peace

I embrace new beginnings with an open heart, knowing that each day is a fresh opportunity to create the life I desire.

CHAPTER THREE

CULTIVATING RESILIENCE

Resilience is the inner strength that enables us to bounce back from adversity and face life's challenges with courage and determination. In the aftermath of a divorce, cultivating resilience is not just a helpful trait – it's a necessity. It's the foundation upon which you can rebuild your life and emerge from this divorce stronger and better than before the marriage.

Resilience is not a fixed trait; it's a skill that can be developed and honed over time. It's the ability to adapt to adversity, cope with stress, and maintain a positive outlook even in difficult circumstances. Understanding that resilience is a process that can help you approach divorce with patience and perseverance.

Resilience does not mean suppressing your emotions or pretending that everything is fine. It means acknowledging your feelings and allowing yourself to grieve the end of your marriage. Divorce often brings a mix of emotions: sadness, anger, fear, and confusion. It's essential to process these emotions rather than bottle them up. Seek the support of a therapist or a support group if needed to help you navigate this emotional terrain.

One of the key elements of resilience is having a strong support network. Surround yourself with people who offer emotional support, encouragement, and a listening ear.

Trusted friends and family members can play a significant role in helping you build resilience. They can provide perspective, offer guidance, and remind you that you're not alone on this journey.

Resilience involves the ability to tackle challenges head-on. Develop problem-solving skills to adjust the practical issues that may arise during and after divorce, such as financial adjustments, co-parenting arrangements, or finding stable housing. Seek professional advice or guidance when necessary to navigate these challenges effectively.

A positive mindset is a crucial aspect of resilience. It's not about denying the difficulties you face but rather focusing on your strengths, opportunities, and the possibility of growth.

Cultivate a habit of positive self-talk and remind yourself of your accomplishments and capabilities. Surround yourself with inspirational quotes and affirmations or create a gratitude journal to help maintain a positive perspective.

Taking care of your physical and emotional well-being is foundational to resilience. Ensure you sleep well, maintain a healthy diet, and exercise regularly.

Self-care activities such as meditation, mindfulness, or relaxation techniques can help reduce stress and build resilience. Remember that self-care isn't selfish; it's a necessary investment in your resilience. Resilience involves setting realistic goals and breaking them down into manageable steps.

By achieving small victories along the way, you can build your confidence and sense of control. Celebrate your accomplishments, no matter how minor they seem, as they contribute to your overall resilience. Resilience is not just about bouncing back but also about growing stronger through adversity.

View your divorce as a learning experience. Reflect on the lessons you've gained about yourself, relationships, and what you want from life. Use these insights to make informed decisions and to shape your future in a way that aligns with your values and aspirations.

Cultivating resilience is an ongoing process that requires patience and self-compassion. It's about developing the inner strength to navigate the challenges that come your way and emerge from them as a more resilient and empowered individual. Remember that resilience is not about avoiding adversity but facing it with courage, believing that you have the inner resources to overcome it.

Affirmations of Peace

I am resilient, and I can overcome any challenge that comes my way.

Section II:

SOULFUL HEALING

"But if the unbelieving depart, let him depart. A brother or a sister is not under bondage in such cases: but God hath called us to peace."

(1 Cor 7:15, KJV)

CHAPTER FOUR

REDISCOVERING INDEPENDENCE

Divorce often marks a significant shift in your life, especially regarding your sense of independence. Rediscovering and nurturing your independence are crucial in your journey toward post-divorce empowerment and personal growth. Let's explore the importance of independence, as guidance is offered on regaining and celebrating it.

One of the immediate changes of divorce is regaining personal freedom. You no longer must consider someone else's needs, desires, or opinions in your daily decisions. This newfound freedom can be liberating and an opportunity to rediscover who you are as an individual. Embrace the chance to make choices that align with your values and interests.

Rediscovering independence often involves a journey of self-discovery and self-identity. During a marriage, it's common for some aspects of your individuality to become intertwined with your partner's.

Take this time to reconnect with your core values, beliefs, interests, and passions that may have been neglected or overlooked. Reflect on what truly makes you unique and what brings you joy.

Financial independence is a crucial aspect of personal anatomy. After divorce, you may need to reassess your financial situation and adjust accordingly. Create a budget, set financial goals, and work on securing your financial future. Knowing that you can manage your finances independently and make decisions that align with your financial well-being is empowering.

While independence is essential, it doesn't mean you must do it alone. Building a support system of family and friends is vital during this period of rediscovery. A reliable support network can provide emotional encouragement, guidance, and a sense of security as you embark on your journey toward independence.

Establishing healthy boundaries is a crucial part of rediscovering independence. This includes setting boundaries with your ex-husband , with whom you may still interact with and others in your life. Clear boundaries help protect your emotional well-being and ensure that your decisions and actions are aligned with your personal goals.

Independence also means taking the initiative in your life. Make proactive choices that empower you and move you closer to your goals. Whether it's pursuing new career opportunities, deciding about your living arrangements, or taking up new hobbies and interests. Taking the lead in your life helps you regain a sense of control and purpose.

A divorce can sometimes cause isolation or a disrupted social life. Rediscovering independence often involves reconnecting with your social circle. Rekindle old friendships and cultivate new ones. Engage in social activities and events that align with your interests, helping you build a fulfilling and active social life.

Self-reliance is a core component of independence. It means developing the skills and confidence to handle life challenges independently. Embrace opportunities to learn new skills, from practical tasks like managing finances to emotional skills like coping with stress and adversity. The more self-reliant you become, the more empowered you will feel.

Rediscovering independence is a journey marked by milestones, no matter how small they may seem. Celebrate these achievements as they come. They represent your growth and progress. Acknowledging your milestones forces your sense of autonomy and remind you of your strength and resilience.

Rediscovering independence after divorce is a transformative process that allows you to regain control of your life, redefine your identity, and pursue your happiness and fulfillment. It's about recognizing your interests and strengths and embracing the opportunities that come with newfound freedom. By taking proactive steps and nurturing your independence, you can survive post-divorce and thrive in a life that is uniquely yours.

Affirmations of Peace

I am capable and self-reliant, and I embrace my independence within.

CHAPTER FIVE

REBUILDING YOUR LIFE

After a divorce, rebuilding your life can be daunting but ultimately rewarding. Let's focus on the steps and strategies to rebuild various aspects of your life, from your personal well-being to your social connections. It's a process of self-discovery, growth, and transformation.

I had previously set goals that aligned with being married with three children. One day, I realized that I was now a single mother with three children. This time, I needed to set goals that would meet the needs of my new life.

The first step in rebuilding your life after divorce is honestly accessing your current situation. Take stock of where you are emotionally, financially, and socially. Understand the changes that have occurred and the challenges you may face. This self-awareness forms the foundation for your rebuilding efforts.

Rebuilding your life begins with setting clear, achievable goals. These goals can encompass various aspects of your life, such as your career, personal development, social life, and well-being. Specific objectives provide direction and motivation for your journey.

Divorce can take a toll on your physical and emotional well-being. Prioritize self-care as you rebuild your life. This includes eating healthy, getting regular exercise, and managing stress effectively. Self-care isn't just about pampering yourself; it's about maintaining the energy and resilience needed for rebuilding.

Rebuilding your life may involve complex legal, financial, or emotional issues. Don't hesitate to seek professional guidance when needed. Consult with therapists, financial advisors, or career counselors who can provide expert advice tailored to your specific circumstances.

Social connections are vital for emotional support and personal growth. Reconnect with old friends, make new ones, and nurture meaningful relationships. Join social groups or organizations that align with your interests to expand your social network.

If you have children, navigating co-parenting arrangements is essential to rebuilding your life. Maintain open communication with your ex-husband , prioritize your children's well-being, and work together to create a stable and supportive environment for them.

Rebuilding your career after divorce may involve making changes or pursuing new opportunities. Update your resume, explore additional training or education, and network within your industry. Consider whether a career change is right for you and take the steps necessary to pursue it.

Financial stability is a crucial aspect of rebuilding your life. Create a budget, set financial goals, and work on rebuilding your savings and investments. Seek financial advice to help you make informed decisions and secure your financial future.

Rebuilding your life can also allow you to explore new hobbies and interests. Pursuing activities you're passionate about brings joy, introduces you to like-minded individuals, and expands your horizons. Rebuilding your life is a journey of change and growth. Embrace the process, understanding that it may have its ups and downs.

Mistakes and setbacks are a natural part of the process and can be valuable learning experiences. Flexibility is essential as you rebuild your life because circumstances may change. Be open to adjusting your goals and plans as needed. Your priorities and aspirations may evolve as you progress on your journey.

Throughout your rebuilding journey, take time to celebrate your achievements, no matter how small they may seem. Recognize your progress and the resilience it took to get where you are. Celebrating achievements reinforces your sense of accomplishment and motivates you to keep moving forward.

Rebuilding your life after divorce is a transformative process that allows you to create a future that aligns with your values and aspirations. It's about finding your strengths, resilience, and ability to thrive in the face of adversity. By setting clear goals, prioritizing self-care, seeking support when needed, and embracing change, you can rebuild a life that is not only fulfilling but also uniquely yours.

Affirmations of Peace

I am the architect of my life, and I am rebuilding it with purpose and determination. Each step I take is a step toward a bigger, brighter future.

CHAPTER SIX

FINDING YOUR INNER STRENGTH

Divorce can test your emotional and mental resilience like a few other life events. Explore the process of finding and nurturing your inner strength as you navigate the challenges and changes that come with divorce. Your inner strength is a well of resilience, courage, and determination that can help you not only survive but thrive during this transformation period.

Inner strength is often described as the ability to withstand adversity, overcome challenges, and maintain a positive attitude in the face of difficulties. It's not an innate trade that some people have, and others don't; instead, it's a quality that can be developed and cultivated over time.

A key aspect of finding inner strength is accepting vulnerability. It's okay to acknowledge your emotional pain, fears, and insecurities during and after divorce. In fact, recognizing your vulnerabilities is a crucial step toward building resilience. Only by acknowledging these feelings can you address them and ultimately grow stronger.

Self-compassion is a vital component of inner strength. Treat yourself with the same kindness and understanding you would offer a close friend facing a difficult situation. Engage in self-care practices that nourish your physical, emotional, and mental well-being. This can include meditation, mindfulness, exercise, and seeking therapy or counseling if needed.

The way you speak to yourself internally can significantly impact your inner strength. Replace negative self-talk with positive affirmations and constructive thoughts. See yourself the way that God sees you. The Bible says that death and life is in the power of the tongue. Speak life over your goals and into your children.

Challenge self-doubt and replace it with self-belief. Affirmations like "I am strong," "I am resilient," and "I can handle this" can help reinforce your inner strength.

Finding inner strength doesn't mean you have to go it alone; seek support from friends, family, support groups, a therapist, or a pastor. Sharing your thoughts and feelings with others can provide valuable perspectives, encouragement, and a sense of connection during challenging times.

Setting healthy boundaries is an integral part of cultivating inner strength. Boundaries protect your emotional well-being and help you maintain control over your life. Be clear about what you will and won't tolerate in your interactions with others, including your ex-husband . This clarity can reduce stress and empower you to make choices that align with your values.

Resilience-building practices, such as mindfulness, meditation, and journaling, can help you connect with your inner strength. These practices encourage self-reflection, self-awareness, and emotional regulation. They can also reduce stress and anxiety, allowing you to navigate the challenges of divorce more effectively.

Finding inner strength often involves seeking personal growth. Embrace opportunities for learning and self-improvement. This could include taking up new hobbies, pursuing educational goals, or attending workshops and seminars that align with your interests and aspirations. After my divorce, I returned to college. I earned a bachelors, a masters, and a doctorate degree.

Reflect on past experiences where you demonstrated inner strength and resilience. These instances can serve as reminders of your capacity to overcome adversity. Remember the challenges you faced and how you emerged from them, as they can be a source of inspiration and motivation. Maintaining a positive outlook and focusing on the future can help you tap into your inner strength.

Visualize the life you want to create post-divorce and set goals to achieve that vision. By concentrating on your goals and aspirations, you can harness your inner strength to propel you forward.

Celebrating your progress in small victories along the way. Each step forward is a testament to your inner strength. Recognize your resilience and your ability to adapt and thrive in the face of adversity. Celebrating these accomplishments reinforces your sense of inner strength and self-worth.

Finding your inner strength during and after divorce is an ongoing journey of self-discovery and personal growth. It's about acknowledging your vulnerabilities while recognizing your resilience and capacity for growth. By practicing self-compassion, seeking support, setting boundaries, and focusing on your personal growth, you can tap into your inner strength and use it as a powerful resource to navigate the challenges of divorce and create a brighter future.

It's important to note that everyone's journey is unique, and finding strength in God after divorce is a personal experience. It may involve a combination of the above strategies or other practices that resonate with one's faith and beliefs. It's also essential to be patient with oneself and allow for healing and spiritual growth.

Trust in the Lord and lean not on your own understanding. Sometimes, when we're in a relationship, we talk to other people. But one thing we must do is trust in the Lord. We must allow God to lead and guide us in the way that we should go.

Often, we see other people's relationships and how they handle their marriage or divorce, but we must put our trust in God. We must allow God to show us because only God knows what the future holds. God knows what's before us, what we're going through, and what we will go through, and we must trust Him when we can't see the full stairway.

We must trust God when we can't see the miles ahead of us; we must trust God and know that because we are a child of God, He will guide us in the right direction. He will place our footsteps one step in front of the other and show us what we need to do to make it.

Finding strength in God after divorce is a transformational journey that encompasses both the emotional and spiritual realms. Divorce can be a profoundly challenging experience, leaving us feeling broken, lost, and overwhelmed. In these moments of vulnerability, turning to your faith and seeking solace in God's presence can provide a powerful source of strength and healing.

Prayer becomes a lifeline for those navigating the stormy seas of divorce. It's not merely a ritual; it's a heartfelt conversation with the divine. In prayer, we pour out our pain, confusion, and fears while finding comfort in the belief that God listens and understands. As we surrender our burdens to a higher power, a profound sense of relief washes over us, allowing us to breathe more freely and find a glimmer of hope in the darkness.

Seeking spiritual guidance takes on new significance during this tumultuous time. Pastors and counselors offer a steady hand and compassionate ear, guiding us toward a deeper understanding of their faith teachings and principles. They help unravel the complexities of divorce, offering insights and wisdom that align with their spiritual beliefs. These mentors become beacons of light, illuminating a path toward healing and spiritual growth.

Active participation in religious and congregational activities fosters a sense of community and belonging.
Within the sacred walls of a place of worship, we find spiritual substance and a supportive community of like-minded believers. Coming together to worship and pray, surrounded by others who may have faced similar trials, reinforces our faith and provides a refuge from the world's chaos.

As we dwell on the passages, we uncover pearls of wisdom that resonate with our own experiences, offering a sense of connection with those who have faced adversity before us.

In the company of support groups specifically tailored for those of us going through divorce, we as individuals can find a safe space to share our stories, fears, and triumphs. These groups become a circle of empathy and encouragement where we can give and receive support. In the shared experiences of others, we see a glimpse of our own strength and resilience.

Volunteering and engaging in acts of charity become avenues for channeling the pain of divorce into a force for good. By helping others in need, we find purpose and meaning in our faith, shifting the focus from personal challenges to positively impacting the world. In serving others, we discover that we are not defined by our divorce but by our capacity for love and kindness.

Forgiveness, a central tenet in many religions, becomes a pivotal step in the journey toward healing. Whether seeking forgiveness from God or oneself, it is a transformative act that unburdens the heart and allows room for growth and renewal. Letting go of resentment and bitterness paves the way for inner peace and spiritual strength.

Journaling and reflection provide a therapeutic outlet for processing complex emotions and seeking clarity in one's faith journey. You can document your thoughts, prayers, and moments of insight through the written word. This practice records your evolving relationship with God, serving as a testament to your resilience and spiritual growth.

The support of friends and family who share your faith and values becomes a source of immense comfort and companionship. These loved ones offer unwavering emotional support, standing by your side as you navigate the tumultuous waters of divorce. Together, you find strength in the bonds of faith and the solidarity of family and friends.

Finding strength through God during divorce is a deeply personal and transformational process. It involves prayer, seeking spiritual guidance, participating in religious communities, studying sacred texts, connecting with support groups, engaging in acts of service, embracing forgiveness, journaling, and leaning on the support of loved ones.

This multifaceted journey leads us from a place of brokenness to a place of spiritual strength, reminding us that we are never alone, even in the face of life's greatest challenges. Your faith can be a wellspring of resilience and renewal.

Affirmations of Peace

I draw strength from within, tapping into my inner resilience and courage. I am strong, capable, and I trust God to bring me through stronger than I was before.

CHAPTER SEVEN

EMOTIONAL ROLLER COASTERS

Divorce is undeniably an emotional roller coaster. The process can evoke a wide range of feelings, from anger and sadness to relief and confusion. Coping with these emotional ups and downs is essential for your well-being during and after divorce.

You might find that some days you are stronger than other days. I remember the first Thanksgiving after my divorce. I just didn't feel happy. I knew that I was thankful for my children, but I couldn't find my joy.

Let's explore strategies to help you navigate the emotional turbulence often accompanying divorce.

Allow yourself to grieve. Grief is a natural response to the loss of a marriage. It's essential to allow yourself to grieve and process the emotions that come with it. Recognize that grief is not a linear process, and it's okay to experience various emotions at different times.

Seek emotional support. Share your feelings with trusted friends and family who can help lift your spirits. This support system can provide a safe space to express your emotions and receive empathy and understanding. Don't hesitate to reach out for help when needed.

Practice self-compassion. Be kind and patient with yourself. Self-compassion involves treating yourself with the same understanding and care you would offer a friend in a similar situation. Avoid self-blame and negative self-talk, as they can exacerbate emotional distress.

Mindfulness and meditation. Mindfulness techniques and meditation can help you stay grounded and centered during emotional turmoil. These practices encourage you to be present in the moment, observe your emotions without judgment, and manage stress effectively.

Maintain healthy habits. Taking care of your physical well-being is closely tied to your emotional health. Ensure you get enough sleep, eat a balanced diet, and exercise regularly. These habits can help regulate your mood and provide resilience against emotional mood swings.

Journaling. Writing down your thoughts and feelings in a journal can be a therapeutic way to process your emotions. It allows you to gain clarity, track your progress, and identify reoccurring patterns in your emotional responses.

Establish clear boundaries. Minimize unnecessary emotional triggers by establishing clear boundaries with your ex-husband . Determine what level of communication and interaction is necessary and healthy for both parties and stick to those boundaries.

If you have children, co-parenting can be emotionally challenging but also an opportunity for collaboration and support. Keep the kids' well-being in mind and maintain a cooperative and respectful co-parenting relationship with your ex-husband.

Create a supportive routine. A structured daily routine can provide stability and a sense of control during tumultuous times. Include self-care activities, work, social interactions, and time for hobbies or interests that bring you joy.

Embrace change. Recognize that divorce represents a significant change in your life. Embrace change as an opportunity for personal growth and transformation. Focus on the possibilities and new beginnings that lie ahead.

Practice emotional resilience. Emotional resilience involves adapting to adversity and bouncing back from challenges. Develop resilience by learning from your emotional experiences, building coping strategies, and maintaining a positive outlook.

Consider professional help. If you find it difficult to maintain your emotions or if they interfere with your daily life, consider seeking professional help from a therapist, pastor, or counselor. They can provide strategies and support to navigate complex emotions.

Focus on the future. While it's important to acknowledge and process your emotions, don't get stuck in the past. Shift your focus towards the future and the opportunities it holds. Set goals and aspirations that give you a sense of purpose and direction.

Celebrate small victories. Acknowledge and celebrate your small victories along the way. Each step forward, no matter how small, is a testament to your resilience and strength. Celebrating these accomplishments can boost your self-esteem and motivation.

Coping with the emotional roller coaster of divorce is a challenging journey, but it can lead to personal growth and healing. Remember that healing takes time, and it's okay to seek help when needed. By practicing self-compassion, seeking support, and developing resilience, you can navigate the emotional turbulence of divorce and emerge from it stronger and more emotionally resilient.

Affirmations of Peace

I honor my emotions and navigate them with grace and resilience in the face of emotional challenges.

Section III:

COURAGE TO BLOSSOM

"But thanks be to God, which giveth us the victory through our Lord Jesus Christ."

(1 Corinthians 15:57)

CHAPTER EIGHT

SELF-CARE AND WELLNESS

Self-care and wellness are paramount when navigating life after a divorce. Let's dive into the importance of prioritizing your physical and emotional well-being, offering guidance on practicing self-care, and nurturing your overall wellness during this transformation.

1. Prioritizing Self-Care
Divorce can be emotionally draining, making self-care essential. Prioritizing self-care means dedicating time and attention to your physical, emotional, and mental health. It's about recognizing that taking care of yourself is not selfish; it's a necessary act of self-perseveration.

2. Physical Self-Care
Physical self-care involves maintaining your physical health. This includes:
· Regular exercise: engaging in physical activity promotes physical health and releases endorphins, boosting your mood and reducing stress.

·   Healthy eating: a balanced diet provides the nutrients your body and mind need to function optimally. Avoid excessive consumption of comfort foods or emotional eating, which can be tempting during challenging times.

Adequate sleep: prioritize sleep to ensure you're well-rested and can maintain stress effectively. Lack of sleep can exacerbate emotional distress.

3. Emotional Self-Care
Emotional self-care centers on managing your emotions and nurturing your emotional well-being. This includes:

·   Expressing emotions: allow yourself to feel and express your emotions without judgment. Journaling, talking to a trusted friend, or seeking therapy can help you process your feelings.

·   Mindfulness and meditation: these practices can help you stay present in the moment, reduce anxiety, and manage emotional reactions more effectively.

·   Seeking professional support: if you're struggling with overwhelming emotions or mental health issues, consider seeking the help of a therapist, pastor or counselor.

4. Mental Self-Care

Mental self-care involves nurturing your cognitive and intellectual well-being. This includes:

· Continuous learning: engaging in activities that challenge your mind, such as learning a new skill, pursuing educational interests, or reading, can stimulate mental growth and resilience.

· Stress management: develop stress management techniques, such as deep breathing exercises, visualization, or relaxation practices, to help you cope with the emotional upheaval.

5. Social Self-Care

Social self-care focuses on your interactions with others and the relationships contributing to your well-being. This includes:

· Building a support network: surround yourself with friends and family who offer emotional support and understanding.

· Setting boundaries: establish clear boundaries in your relationship to protect your emotional health and prevent undue stress.

· Engaging in social activities: participate in social activities or join clubs and groups that align with your interests, helping you build meaningful connections.

6. Spiritual Self-Care

Spiritual self-care centers nurture your sense of purpose, meaning, and connection to something greater than yourself. This can involve: Spiritual practices: engage in activities that resonate with your spiritual beliefs, such as meditation, prayer, or attending religious services.

· Self-reflection: take time for introspection and self-discovery to clarify your values, beliefs, and life purpose.

7. Creating a Self-Care Routine

Make self-care a consistent part of your life, and create a self-care routine tailored to your needs and preferences. Schedule self-care activities into your daily or weekly calendar, treating them as non-negotiable appointments with yourself.

8. Celebrate Small Achievements

Acknowledge and celebrate your self-care achievements. Every step you take to prioritize your well-being is a victory. Recognizing and celebrating those achievements can motivate you to continue investing in self-care and wellness.

9. Seek Professional Help When Needed

If you find it challenging to incorporate self-care into your life or if you're struggling with emotional distress, don't hesitate to seek professional help. Therapists, pastors, counselors, and wellness professionals can provide guidance and support tailored to your needs.

10. Embrace Holistic Wellness

Remember that self-care and wellness are holistic, encompassing your life's physical, emotional, mental, social, and spiritual aspects. Balance and integration among these areas are vital to nurturing your overall well-being.

Self-care and wellness are important components of navigating life after divorce. By prioritizing your physical, emotional, and mental health, you can not only cope with the challenges of divorce but also emerge from stronger and more resilient. Recognize that self-care is an ongoing practice, and your commitment to it is an investment in your long-term well-being and happiness.

Affirmation of Peace

I prioritize self-care and wellness in my life. Taking care of myself is an act of self-love and self-respect.

CHAPTER NINE

CELEBRATING YOUR TRIUMPHS

Always believe that God does not give us more than we can handle. I always believe that we are more than conquerors. Many of us go through negative, traumatic situations in our lives, but God is always there. When we face traumatic situations, God is right there with us. He carries us through those situations, and I've heard it said that God will never give you more than you can bear. I heard it said, when you trust God, He will help you through all situations.

The Bible says in John 1:2, to count it all joy when you go through trials and tribulations. No, it's not a joyful time. It's not a joyful situation, but you count it all joy because you know God is about to take you to another level. God is about to elevate you and open doors that have never been opened.

We go through trials and tests, and we go through uncomfortable situations. God is showing you that He will get you through this, you must get through this, and you must climb this mountain. On the other side of this mountain, there's glory, there's greatness, there's success.

So, when you're going through it, you don't want to stop; you want to keep climbing because you are more than a conqueror. When you get to the other side, you'll look back, and you'll see why you had to go through the things that you went through. No, it's not a pleasant time, but it's a time of testimony. It's a time for you to grow in the Lord and grow in Christ. We are here to share with the next young lady what we went through so that she can get through it as well.

Celebrating your triumphs is a pivotal chapter in this journey through life after divorce. It's about recognizing your resilience, acknowledging your achievements, and embracing the growth and transformation that have emerged from the challenges you've faced.

The significance of celebrating your triumphs, offers guidance on how to do so in a meaningful and empowering way. The importance of celebration is a way of honoring yourself and your journey. It's a means of validating your efforts and acknowledging your progress.

You may have faced emotional, financial, and personal challenges in the aftermath of a divorce, but celebrating your triumph can remind you of your strength and resilience, boost your self-esteem, and reinforce a positive self-image.

Embrace self-appreciation. Celebrating your triumphs begins with self-appreciation. Recognize that you deserve acknowledgment and celebration. Your journey through divorce may have been difficult, but it's also a testament to your inner strength and courage.

Practice self-compassion. Treat yourself with kindness and understanding. Celebrate your achievements with the same enthusiasm and encouragement you would offer a close friend. **Cultivate positive self-talk.** Challenge negative self-talk and self-doubt with positive affirmations. Remind yourself of your resilience and your capabilities.

Reflect on your journey. Take time to reflect on your journey after divorce. Consider how far you've come and the challenges you've overcome. Reflecting on your experiences can provide valuable insights and a sense of gratitude.

Journaling. Write down your thoughts and feelings about your journey. Document the highs and lows, the lessons you've learned, and the personal growth you've achieved.

Visualization. Visualize the path you've traveled and envision your future. Imagine the possibilities and opportunities that lie ahead due to your triumphs.

Set milestones and goals. Celebrate your triumphs by setting milestones and goals. These can be both short-term and long-term achievements that reflect your progress and aspirations.

Having clear objectives provides direction and motivation for your journey. Create a vision board and compile images, quotes, and symbols representing your goals and aspirations. Display your vision board in a permanent place to remind yourself of what you're working toward.

Acknowledge small victories. Don't underestimate the significance of small victories. Each step forward, no matter how minor it may seem, is a triumph worth celebrating.

Share your triumph. Sharing your triumph with others can enhance the celebration experience. It invites support, validation, and connections with loved ones who have been part of your journey. Celebrate with loved ones, and invite friends and family to join in your celebration. Share your achievements and milestones with those who have supported you along the way.

Join support groups. Consider joining support groups or communities of individuals who have experienced divorce. Sharing your triumphs with those who can relate can be particularly rewarding.

Plan meaningful celebrations. Celebrating your triumphs doesn't have to be extravagant; it should be meaningful to you. Plan celebrations that resonate with your values and interests.

Personal rituals. Create personal rituals or traditions to mark your triumphs. This could involve lighting a candle, writing a letter to yourself, or taking a meaningful trip.

Symbolic gestures. Choose symbols or items that represent your achievements. Wear a piece of jewelry, display a meaningful object, or plant a tree to commemorate your triumphs.

Pay it forward. Consider using your triumphs as an opportunity to give back or support others who are going through similar challenges. Sharing your experiences and stories can inspire and empower others on their journey.

Mentorship. Offer mentorship or guidance to individuals facing divorce or other life challenges. Your wisdom and resilience can serve as a source of inspiration and support.

Cultivate a gratitude practice. Incorporate gratitude into your celebration process. Recognize the people, opportunities, and circumstances contributing to your triumphs. A gratitude practice can enhance your sense of fulfillment and well-being.

A gratitude journal. Keep a journal where you regularly write down things that you're grateful for, including your triumphs in the positive aspects of your life. Keep celebrating your triumphs as an ongoing practice.

Your journey in life after divorce is not limited to a single chapter; it's a continuous evolution. Embrace each new triumph as a steppingstone to a new chapter of your life. Celebrating your triumphs is essential to healing, growth, and empowerment in life after divorce. It's a way to acknowledge your resilience, honor your journey, and embrace the possibilities that lie ahead.

By cultivating self-appreciation, reflecting on your journey, setting meaningful goals, sharing with loved ones, planning meaningful celebrations, paying it forward, practicing gratitude, and maintaining a continuous celebration mindset, you can infuse your life with a sense of fulfillment and empowerment that carries you forward into a bright and promising future.

Affirmations of Peace

I celebrate my triumphs, both big and small. Each accomplishment is a testament to my strength and my resilience.

CHAPTER TEN

RECONNECTING WITH YOUR PASSIONS

One of the most transformative opportunities that come with life after divorce is the chance to rediscover and reignite your passions and interests. Let's explore the significance of reconnecting with your passions and provide guidance on how to embark on this journey of self-discovery and personal fulfillment.

Passions are the things that ignite your soul, bring joy to your heart, and give life meaning and purpose. They are the activities, hobbies, or pursuits that make you feel most like yourself and connect you to your authentic essence. After a divorce, when you may have lost a part of your identity within the context of your marriage, rediscovering your passions can be a powerful way to rebuild your sense of self and find fulfillment.

1. Self-discovery. Reconnecting with your passion is an opportunity for self-discovery. It's a chance to explore who you are beyond your role as a spouse or partner consider the following steps:

· Reflect on your past interests: think back to activities or hobbies that once brought you joy. What did you enjoy doing before your marriage or during the early stages of your life together?

Try new things: be open to experimenting with new activities and experiences. You may discover previously unknown passions that resonate with your current self.

·   Seek inspiration: explore books, magazines, blogs, or social media related to your potential areas of interest. Exposure to new ideas can spark passion and creativity.

2. Making time for your passions

Reconnecting with your passions requires dedicating time and energy to them. Here's how to incorporate your passions into your post-divorce life:

·   Create a schedule: blackout specific times in your calendar for activities that align with your passions. Treat these appointments with the same importance as any other commitments. Start small: if you have limited time or energy, begin with small, manageable steps. Even spending just a few minutes a day on a passion project can be rewarding.

 Prioritize self-care: remember that pursuing your passion is a form of self-care. It nurtures your soul, reduces stress, and enhances your overall well-being.

3. Overcoming challenges

Reconnecting with your passions may come with challenges, especially if you've set them aside for a long time. Here's how to address common obstacles:

- Self-doubt: if you doubt your abilities or feel you've lost touch with your passions, be patient with yourself.

Reconnecting is a journey, and progress takes time.
- Lack of resources: some passions may require resources like time, money, or equipment. Consider creative solutions, such as borrowing or sharing resources with others who share your interests.

- Balancing responsibilities: finding time for your passion may be challenging when balancing work, family, and other responsibilities. Prioritize self-care, communicate your needs with loved ones, and delegate tasks when possible.

4. Pursuing growth and fulfillment

Reconnecting with your passions is not just about indulging and enjoyable activities; it's also about personal growth and fulfillment:

- Passion-driven goals: set goals related to your passions that challenge you to learn, grow, and achieve. Whether mastering a new skill, completing a project, or reaching a personal milestone, these goals can provide a sense of purpose and achievement.

Rebuilding connections: pursuing your passion can also lead to meaningful connections with like-minded individuals. Join clubs, groups, and communities related to your interest to expand your social network.

5. Celebrating your journey
Throughout your journey of rediscovering your passions, take time to celebrate your progress and achievements. Each step you take towards reigniting your passion is a victory.

- Recognize that your passions are integral to your identity and can bring joy and fulfillment to your life.

Reconnecting with your passions is a powerful way to navigate life after divorce. It's an opportunity for self-discovery, personal growth, and a deep sense of fulfillment. Embrace this journey with an open heart, be patient with yourself, and allow your passions to rekindle the flames of your inner joy and authenticity. In the process, you're healed from the past and embrace the exciting possibilities of your future.

Affirmations of Peace

I am passionate about life, and I embrace my interests and hobbies. Reconnecting with my passions bring joy and fulfillment.

CHAPTER ELEVEN

HEALING WITHIN

As the dust settled on the life I once knew, I was left standing in the rubble of not just a broken marriage but a fractured sense of self. It was then that I realized healing would not come from external sources. It had to start from within. We'll explore the internal healing process, a path marked by introspection, acceptance, and gradual rebirth.

Healing from within begins with the daunting task of facing your pain head-on. It's tempting to numb the hurt with distractions or to bury it under the face of "I'm fine," but true healing demands honesty. It requires sitting with your emotions, however uncomfortable or overwhelming, and recognizing them as signposts on your journey. They're not there to torture you but to teach you.

The first step is acknowledgment. Acknowledge the hurt, the betrayal, the disappointment, and the fear. Give yourself permission to grieve not just the loss of your partner but the loss of the future you had envisioned together. Understand that grief is not a linear process. You may cycle through anger, denial, bargaining, depression, and acceptance multiple times. Each cycle is a layer of healing, peeling back the pain to reveal the core of who you are and who you can become.

With acknowledgment comes the need for self-compassion. Be kind to yourself. Speak to yourself with the same empathy and understanding you would offer a dear friend. Remind yourself that healing is not a race; there's no timetable and no shortcut. Each small step forward is worth celebrating.

As you navigate this path, seek tools and practices that resonate with your soul. For some, healing may involve therapy or counseling, providing a safe space to unravel the complex emotions and thoughts that accompany divorce. For some, it may be meditation, yoga, or journaling – practices that encourage mindfulness and self-reflection. And for many, it involves rekindling passions and hobbies that were put aside, rediscovering joy and fulfillment, and doing things just for you.

As you journey inward, you'll redefine your identity separate from your past relationship. You'll discover strength you never knew you had or an interest that excites you.

This is the process of rebuilding, brick by brick, day by day, a life that feels authentic and fulfilling. But perhaps the most profound aspect of healing from within is the realization that you are not broken. You are whole, even in your pain, even in your healing, you are not defined by your divorce or by the past. Instead, you are defined by the courage to show up each day as you rebuild your life.

Let's explore these things more deeply, offering practical advice, personal reflections, and exercises to aid you in your healing journey.

Together, we'll discover the transformative power of healing from within, setting the foundation for a future filled with possibilities, happiness, and an unbroken sense of self.

Healing from within after divorce is a profound journey of self-discovery and renewal. The end of a marriage often leaves emotional scars and a sense of loss. Still, it also provides an opportunity for personal growth and healing.

Another step in the process is self-compassion. It's crucial to acknowledge and validate the pain, grief and mixed emotions that accompany divorce. Instead of suppressing these feelings, learn to embrace them as a natural part of the healing process through self-compassion. Begin to treat yourself with the same kindness and understanding that you would offer to a friend in a similar situation.

Self-reflection plays a pivotal role in this healing journey. It involves deeply examining your own experiences, behaviors, and patterns in the relationship. Introspection allows you to gain valuable insights into yourself and your needs, paving the way for personal growth and healthier future relationships.

Seeking support from friends, family, and pastors is another crucial aspect of healing after divorce. Sharing that emotion with a trusted support network that can provide a sense of connection and relief, can be powerful. Professional counseling can offer tools and strategies to navigate emotional challenges and help individuals rebuild their lives.

Affirmations of Peace

I am at peace with my past, present, and future. I release what no longer serves me.

Section IV:

PIECING BACK THE PEACE

"Delight thyself also in the Lord; and he shall give thee the desires of thine heart. Commit that way unto the Lord; Trust also in him; and he shall bring it to pass."

(Psalm 37: 4–5)

CHAPTER TWELVE

REGAINING PEACE

Finding peace after divorce is a deeply personal and transformative journey. It's about coming to terms with your past, healing emotional wounds, and embracing a sense of inner calm and contentment as you move forward.

I have highlighted the significance of gaining peace after divorce. I offer guidance on how to achieve this profound sense of serenity and well-being.

Peace is a state of inner harmony and tranquility that allows you to navigate life challenges with a sense of calm and resilience. After a divorce, peace becomes a beacon of hope a destination that signifies healing, acceptance, and a return to a fulfilling and balanced life.

Finding peace after divorce can be a transformative journey that brings inner serenity and renewal. Divorce often leaves emotional scars, but it also opens the door to a new chapter in life, where peace becomes attainable through various means.

December 31, 2008. I was at church, and it was around midnight. I realized that there was only one way for me to move on with my life after filing for divorce. I knew that I would need to regain my peace. I had spent the last few months dwelling on and asking myself what I could have done better, what I could have done differently, and if was there any way I could have saved my marriage.

That night, as I sat in church, I realized that I needed peace from everything that happened in the last 16 years. I needed to release the thoughts, I needed to release the pain, I needed to release staying up every night waiting for my ex-husband to come home, and I needed to be free. I knew that peace was a sense of freedom.

That night, December 31, 2008, I put the past 16 years behind me and regained my strength and myself.

January 1, 2009, marked the day I began piecing back the peace. I left everything that had happened, everything that I experienced, every negative thing that happened in my marriage in the year 2008. I lost pictures, friends, and my former in-laws. I did not look back. I did not wonder what "could have been" from that day forward. I moved forward in peace.

I began with a binder notebook that I titled Piecing my life back together tracking system. I wrote titles that included: finances, credit, love, peace, family, and spirituality.

One of the keys to achieving peace after divorce is acceptance. It involves acknowledging the reality of the situation and letting go of resistance to the changes that have occurred. Acceptance doesn't mean condoning the pain or difficulties experienced but recognizing them as part of your history.

Self-care plays a vital role in cultivating peace. Taking time to nurture physical, emotional, and mental well-being becomes a priority. This may involve practicing mindfulness, exercising regularly, maintaining a healthy diet, and seeking counseling or therapy to process emotions and gain clarity.

Forgiveness of yourself and your former partner is a powerful catalyst for peace. Letting go of resentment and bitterness can liberate the heart and mind, allowing room for healing and inner calm. It's a process that may take time but can ultimately lead to a profound sense of tranquility.

Focusing on personal growth and setting new goals can help individuals find a sense of purpose and direction post-divorce. This forward-looking perspective allows you to embrace the future with optimism and confidence, ultimately leading to deep and lasting peace.

1. **Acceptance and Forgiveness**

Achieving peace begins with acceptance and forgiveness. These two elements are interconnected and are foundational to the process of letting go of the past.

- **Acceptance** involves acknowledging the reality of your divorce and its impact on your life. It means facing your emotions, the changes that have occurred, and the future that lies ahead. It's about coming to terms with what is and letting go of resistance to the present moment.

- **Forgiveness** is a profound act of releasing the emotional burden of divorce. It's not about condoning any wrongdoing but freeing yourself from anger, resentment, or blame. Forgiving your ex-husband and ultimately forgiving yourself allows you to move forward unencumbered.

2. **Healing Emotional Wounds**

Healing emotional wounds is a central aspect of finding peace after divorce. Emotional wounds can be deep and may take time to mend, but the journey towards healing is essential.

- **Seeking support:** consider seeking support from a therapist, pastor, or counselor who specializes in divorce-related issues. Professional guidance can provide effective strategies for healing emotional wounds.

- **Self-compassion:** be gentle and compassionate with yourself as you heal. Understand that the process is not linear, and there may be ups and downs. Treat yourself with the same kindness as you would offer to a friend going through a difficult time.

- **Self-care:** continue to prioritize self-care practices that promote emotional well-being. Engage in activities that bring you joy, connect with loved ones, and practice mindfulness to stay present and grounded.

3. **Letting Go of Resentment**

Resentment can be a significant barrier to peace. It's a toxic emotion that can keep you tied to the past and hinder your ability to move forward. Here are some things to help you with letting go of resentment.

- **Mindfulness:** mindfulness practices can help you observe and release resentful thoughts and emotions. By staying present and cultivating self-awareness, you can let go of the grip of resentment.

- **Journaling:** write down your feelings of resentment and explore their origins. This can help you gain clarity and develop a deeper understanding of the emotions you're experiencing.

-

Reframe your perspective and try to see your divorce as an opportunity for growth and self-discovery rather than a source of resentment. Reframing your perspective can shift your focus toward the positive aspects of your journey.

4. Building a Support System

Having a strong support system is crucial for finding peace after divorce. Surround yourself with people who uplift and empower you can be a source of solace and strength.

- **Lean on loved ones:** share your thoughts and feelings with trusted friends and family members. Don't hesitate to reach out for emotional support when needed. Consider joining support groups and communities of individuals who have experienced divorce. These groups can provide a sense of belonging and understanding.

As you gain peace, create a vision for your future. Envision the life you want to build for yourself, and set goals and aspirations that reflect your newfound sense of self and contentment. Gaining peace after divorce is a deeply personal and transformative journey. It's about accepting the past, healing emotional wounds, and embracing a sense of inner calm and contentment as you move forward in your life.

By practicing acceptance and forgiveness, healing emotional wounds, letting go of resentment, building a support system, setting boundaries, rediscovering your identity, cultivating gratitude, embracing the present moment, seeking professional help when needed, and creating a vision for the future, you can embark on a journey of profound self-discovery and inner peace.

Remember that peace is not the absence of challenges but the presence of inner strength and resilience to face life's ups and downs with poise and grace. Regaining your peace also means reclaiming your space. The space we inhabit, both physically and emotionally, are reflections of our inner selves. In the wake of a divorce, these spaces can feel tainted with memories and shared moments, making it challenging to move forward.

Let's discuss cleansing, claiming, and revitalizing these spaces to reflect the new you emerging from the shadows of the past. It's common to feel haunted by the presence of your ex-husband and the shared home or even in your personal spaces. Begin by reimagining these areas – perhaps something as simple as rearranging the furniture or as significant as painting the walls a new color.

Each alteration is subbed towards erasing the old and welcoming the new. Don't underestimate the power of physical changes to bring about emotional shifts. Create a sanctuary that resonates with your newfound independence and joy. Reclaiming your space isn't just about the physical.

It's also about setting boundaries and reclaiming your emotional and social territories. Post-divorce, your relationship and social circles might shift. This is a time to evaluate who uplifts you and who drains you. Surround yourself with people who support and energize you, and don't be afraid to distance yourself from negativity or judgment. Your space extends to the people and the energy you allow into your life.

It's also about reclaiming your time and priorities. Personal priorities often take a back seat during marriage, especially one that ends in divorce. Now is the time to focus on what you want and need.

Take up old hobbies or discover new ones.Travel to places you've dreamt of. Enroll in that class you've always been interested in. This is your time to explore, grow, and indulge in the pleasures that make life meaningful.Emotional spaces are equally crucial. After divorce, you might find yourself inundated with well-meaning advice, questions, or even judgment.

Remember, it's okay to seek solitude and silence when needed. It's okay not to have all the answers or not to want to discuss your journey with everyone. Protecting your emotional space means listening to your needs and honoring them without guilt or explanation.

I delved into strategies for detoxifying and revitalizing your home environment, setting healthy boundaries with others, and prioritizing your own needs and desires. From practical tips on home redecoration to advice on nurturing your emotional well-being, I covered many topics that can help you transform your spaces into reflection on the next version of yourself.

Remember, reclaiming your space is not a one-time event; it is a continuous process of adjusting and reaffirmation. It's about making deliberate choices every day to create and maintain environments that nurture your healing and growth. As you turn the pages, you'll find reflections designed to empower you to take back control of your spaces and begin living your best life.

Affirmation of Peace

I am brave, vulnerable, and authentic in my journey of soulful healing. Each day brings me closer to wholeness and inner peace.

CHAPTER THIRTEEN

NAVIGATING FINANCES

Divorce often brings significant financial changes and challenges, making it crucial to develop a solid understanding of your financial situation and the skills needed to navigate it effectively. I have included strategies and insights to help you take control of your finances during and after divorce.
The first step in navigating finances after divorce is to assess your current financial situation.

This involves taking stock of your assets, debts, income, and expenses. Create a detailed budget to understand your cash flow and identify areas where you need to adjust. Collect all necessary financial documents, including bank statements, tax returns, investment accounts, property deeds, and insurance policies. Having this documentation will be essential for legal and financial planning purposes.

Consider working with a financial advisor or planner who specializes in divorce-related financial matters. They can help you understand your financial options, make informed decisions, and create a long-term financial plan tailored to your post-divorce goals.
Property division is a crucial aspect of divorce, and the laws governing it can vary by jurisdiction.

Familiarize yourself with the property division laws in your area to ensure a fair and equitable distribution of assets and debt. Consulting with an attorney may be necessary to protect your rights and interests. Develop a new budget that reflects your changed circumstances. Account for your solo living expenses, child support or alimony payment, and any other financial obligations. Be realistic about your income and expenses, and prioritize saving for emergencies and long-term goals.

Having an emergency fund is essential for financial security. Strive to save three to six months' worth of living expenses in an easily accessible account to provide a safety net in case you have unexpected financial challenges.

Review and update your legal documents, including your will, trust, beneficiary designations, retirement accounts, and life insurance policies. Ensure that they align with your post-divorce wishes and beneficiaries. Develop a plan to manage and reduce any outstanding debt. Prioritize paying down high-interest debts and consider consolidating or refinancing options to lower interest rates.

Avoid taking on new debts unless it is necessary. Evaluate your health insurance options, especially if you were previously covered under your ex-husband's plan.

Determine if you're eligible for Cobra coverage or explore other insurance options to ensure adequate health coverage. Don't overlook long-term financial planning, including retirement savings. Review your retirement accounts and consider adjusting your contributions to align with your post-divorce financial goals. Consult with a financial advisor to assess your financial readiness.

Keep a close eye on your credit report to ensure that there are no errors or unauthorized accounts. Maintaining good credit is essential for future financial stability. Make sure you understand how your credit score is calculated and take steps to improve it if necessary.

Emotions can run high during divorce proceedings, which may lead to impulsive financial decisions. Take the time to think through major financial choices, such as selling property or dividing assets, to make sure they align with your long-term goals.

Rebuilding your financial independence is a crucial part of post-divorce life. Work towards financial self-sufficiency, even if it takes time to build your career. Exploring additional income sources can contribute to your financial stability.

Don't hesitate to seek support in financial matters. Attend financial workshops, join support groups, or take advantage of resources offered by financial institutions to enhance your financial literacy.

Navigating finances during and after divorce can be challenging. However, you can regain control over your financial future with careful planning and a proactive approach. Remember that seeking professional advice and developing a financial strategy aligned with your goals is crucial to achieving financial security and peace of mind in your new life.

I knew that quitting was not an option. We had gone from a two-parent household with two incomes, and now I was living with my parents and my three children.
Although my parents could provide for us, I was always very independent, and I needed a job.

On September 20, 2008, I went to apply for public assistance. My parents wanted me to stay home with my three children and remain on public assistance. Public assistance said that they would give me $800 a month for me and my three children. I explained to my parents that although I am thankful for public assistance, that is not for me.

I had been in the field of early childhood education for most of my life, and I was in a top position and now I have found myself without a job. I applied for a part-time teacher assistant position, although they would only pay me $700 a month.

On October 13, 2008, I accepted that position. I met my Richard on October 18, 2008. When I say God is working in the background on your behalf, I mean exactly that.

I worked that part-time job for a few months. One day, I was sitting in the classroom, about to read the children a story. I received a call from a lady that had hired me 14 years before that. She said, "Tammy, we need you in our early childhood education program. When can you start?" As much as I wanted to give two weeks' notice to my current job, this new position would pay me three times as much as what I was earning in my current position.

So, I went to my supervisor. It was Friday, and I explained the situation. I said I would not return on Monday because I have a new opportunity. My pay went from $700 a month to $2,200 a month. I worked this job for about 1 year. The current position that I was in, allowed me to be off during the summertime.

So, while I was home, I decided to look and see what other positions were out there. I saw a position that was conducive to my experience and my education. Now, it was the last day to apply for this position. At this time, you had to scan all your documentation along with the application to apply for the position. So, this position was closing at 5:00 PM. I was unfamiliar with using a scanner, so I went to my sister's house to see if my nephew could assist me.

I was not able to get the scanner and everything to work. I said to myself, "You know what? Human resources won't see the documents until Monday anyway, so I'm going to put all my documents in an envelope."

I took my transcripts and my bachelor's degree and the entire application and placed them in the United States postal mail. Again, when I say we serve a mighty God, I mean that. When I say God can take you from the back of the line to the front of the line, that's exactly what I mean.

About a week later, I received a phone call from the school district. The lady on the phone said, "Tammy, I see you tried to apply for a position but all you did was create a profile. But I received your documents in the mail and I will manually put everything in for you."

About two months later I received a phone call. The lady on the phone said, "Your name is going to the Board of Directors tomorrow. If they approve you, you will receive an offer for this position."

I was doing well in my current position; I loved the position that I had, and it wasn't on my mind to move to another position. This position started at $67,300 so when I got off the phone with the lady from human resources, I began to thank God for the position. Remember, I was making $2,200 a month now. I was thanking God because he knew that the children and I needed that level of funds to make it.

God is a provider, Jehovah-Jireh, my provider. When God released me from the marriage that I was in and the financial troubles that I was having, He was showing me that I could trust Him. God basically said, "I got you and these children will be fine." I stayed up most of the night thanking God, praising God, and rejoicing about the position.

The next morning, I went on the website for the school district. I knew that if there was a Board of Directors meeting, then there had to be Board of Director meeting minutes. So, I saw the minutes and read that Tammy Cannon was approved for the position of School Administrator. I owe it all to the Lord.

God can take you out of a situation, where you have no idea why you're being taken out of that position. God began to show me that He had other plans for me. I said to myself, "Lord, I don't know what you have in store for me, but I trust you, and I will sit back and watch it all unfold, because it must be something great.

I gave my two weeks' notice to my current employer. I moved to the city where the position was, and the children and I moved into a very nice apartment across the street from their schools. All three children were within walking distance of their school. God placed us exactly where we needed to be.

One day Richard came to visit me and asked, "How's your credit?" He showed me how to run my credit. I was so embarrassed because my credit after divorce was 504. I took on everything my ex-husband had created in our names. I had 60 pages of charge-offs and late notices, and that day, I realized I needed to make some changes.

In the next few weeks Richard showed me how to rebuild my credit. He taught me how to write letters to the credit bureau and told me what to say to people who would call about late payments. I did everything that he instructed me to do. Today, my credit score is 817.

I began to have the peace that passes all understanding. God elevated me in a way that I could not imagine.

My credit and my finances were better. I paid all the creditors, and so now my credit is better. I found love with Richard. I found stability for myself and my children. I found a church for me and my children, and we were right where God wanted us to be.

Affirmations of Peace

I am in control of my financial well-being. I make wise financial decisions and create a secure future for myself and my children.

CHAPTER FOURTEEN

A LEAP OF FAITH

In the aftermath of divorce, you may feel like your world has shattered into 1000 pieces. The pain, confusion, and headache can be overwhelming. However, this book, Piecing Back the Peace: Life After Divorce, is about embracing a leap of faith and embarking on a journey of soulful healing. It's a journey that leads to the realization that you are not defined by your broken pieces but by your resilience and capacity for transformation.

When a marriage ends, it can feel like a part of your identity has been shattered. The pieces may include your hopes, dreams, shared memories, and even your sense of self. These shattered pieces can leave you feeling lost, broken, and uncertain about the future. However, it's crucial to recognize that even in brokenness, there is potential for growth, strength, and wholeness.

To begin the journey of healing and rediscovering, you must take a leap of faith. A courageous step into the unknown. This leap is an act of self-belief, a declaration that you are willing to gather the fragments of your life and rebuild.
Here are the key components of taking a leap of faith and embracing vulnerability. It means acknowledging your pain, fears, and uncertainties. Allowing yourself to be vulnerable opens the door to authentic healing and transformation.

Be honest with yourself about your feelings. It's okay to grieve, to feel anger, sadness, or even relief. Your emotions are valid and part of the healing process. Share your vulnerabilities with those whom you trust. Their support can provide strength and reassurance during times of uncertainty.

Let go of the past. A leap of faith involves releasing the grip of the past. While your history is integral to your journey, it should not define your future. Forgiving your ex-husband and yourself is a liberating act. It's a conscious decision to release the burdens of blame and resentment. Reflect on the lessons you've gained from your marriage and divorce. What have you learned about yourself, your relationships, and your desires for the future?

Self-compassion is a vital aspect of taking a leap of faith. Treat yourself with the same kindness and understanding you would offer a dear friend facing similar challenges. Challenge and replace negative self-talk with self-compassion affirmations. Remind yourself that you are worthy of love, healing, and happiness. Prioritize self-care practices that nourish your body, mind, and spirit.

Self-care is an act of self-compassion that supports your healing journey. A leap of faith acknowledges that changes are inevitable, and that uncertainty is a part of life. Instead of fearing the unknown, learn to embrace it. Cultivate a mindset of adaptability. Be open to new experiences and opportunities that may arise as you navigate life after divorce. Understand that healing and transformation take time. Embrace the journey, even when progress feels slow or uncertain.

Taking a leap of faith involves setting intentional goals that reflect your desires for the future. As you rebuild your life, these goals serve as beacons of hope and direction. Reflect on your core values and principles. What matters most to you in life? Your goal should align with your values. Break your goals into manageable, actionable steps.

Celebrate each small achievement as you work towards larger aspirations. Resilience is your capacity to bounce back from adversity. A leap of faith recognizes your inner strength and resilience. Reflect on past challenges you've overcome recognize that resilience that already exists within you. Engage in practices that boost your resilience, such as mindfulness, gratitude, and seeking support.

As you take a leap of faith and navigate the path of healing, you embark on a journey of soulful healing. A profound transformation of your inner self that transcends the surface wounds. Soulful healing is about rediscovering your authentic essence, nurturing your spirit, and emerging from adversity with a deeper sense of self-awareness and purpose. Your authentic self is the core of who you are, untarnished by external expectations or past experiences. Soulful healing involves rediscovering and embracing this essence.

Engage in self-reflection, clarify your values, desires, and aspirations. What truly brings you joy and fulfillment? Allow yourself to express your true self, free from the constraints of social norms of others' expectations.

Inner peace is a state of calm and serenity that arises from within. It's a sense of tranquility that transcends external circumstances. Practice mindfulness and meditation to cultivate inner peace. These practices allow you to stay present and centered. Release attachment to external outcomes or material possessions. True peace comes from within and is not dependent on external validation. Self-love is an abounding documental aspect of soulful healing. It's about treating yourself with the same love and care you would offer someone you deeply cherish.

Taking a leap of faith after divorce is a courageous and transformative act, often marked by a profound sense of self-discovery and personal growth. Divorce can make individuals feel broken and uncertain about their future.

However, it also represents an opportunity for reinvention and embracing new possibilities. Taking the leap of faith is to confront fear and uncertainty head-on. Divorce can shake one sense of security, but it also provides a blank canvas upon which to paint a new life. Facing the unknown with resilience and determination is the essence of this leap.

Rediscovering one's identity is a crucial aspect of this journey. After divorce, you often grapple with trust issues, but learning to trust yourself is another step in taking a leap of faith. It involves making decisions that align with your values, aspirations, and innermost desires.

Embracing change and being open to new experiences is fundamental. A leap of faith often involves stepping out of your comfort zone and embracing the unfamiliar. It might mean pursuing a new career, exploring new hobbies, or considering new relationships. Ultimately, taking a leap of faith after divorce is about reclaiming your own narrative and shaping a future filled with hope and purpose.

It's about acknowledging that, despite the pain and challenges, a world of possibilities is waiting to be explored. This leap signifies a bold declaration of self-worth and resilience. It paves the way for a brighter, more fulfilling chapter in life.

Affirmations of Peace

I am a beacon of light and love, radiating compassion and empathy toward myself and others. My journey of soulful healing continues to unfold.

CHAPTER FIFTEEN

REGAINING TRUST

Regaining trust after divorce is a challenging and deeply personal journey that requires time, self-reflection, and a commitment to healing. Divorce often shakes the foundation of trust in yourself and others, as it can be accompanied by feelings of betrayal, hurt, and emotional wounds. However, it is possible to rebuild trust and move forward with a renewed sense of confidence in yourself and future relationships.

The journey of regaining trust begins with introspection and self-acceptance. It's crucial to acknowledge the emotions that accompany divorce: pain, anger, grief, and confusion. By confronting these feelings, you can take the first step towards understanding yourself and the reasons behind the dissolution of your marriage.

Self-acceptance involves forgiving yourself for any perceived mistakes or shortcomings and recognizing that divorce is a complex and often unavoidable life event.

Therapy or counseling can be an invaluable resource for regaining trust after divorce. Trained therapists provide a safe and non-judgmental space to explore emotions, confront past traumas, and develop strategies for rebuilding trust. Through guided sessions, you can gain insights into your thoughts and behaviors, enabling you to work on stress-related issues.

In future relationships, open and honest communication is paramount. Learning to express your feelings, needs, and concerns openly and honestly fosters transparency and builds trust. It's essential to have candid discussions with potential partners about past experiences and how they may impact the future. Being vulnerable and receptive to your partner's communication also contributes to rebuilding trust.

Rebuilding trust takes time and patience. It's crucial to set realistic expectations for yourself and any new relationships that may develop. Trust is not an instantaneous process. It develops gradually as you learn to rely on your own judgment and assess the trustworthiness of others.

Avoid comparing new relationships to the past and allow each connection to evolve naturally. Establishing and maintaining healthy boundaries is vital in the journey to regaining trust.

Clearly defining personal boundaries and communicating them to others helps create a sense of safety and predictability. Respecting your own boundaries and honoring those of your partner is essential for rebuilding trust. Boundaries act as social safeguards against potential breaches of trust.

Caring for your physical and emotional well-being is crucial during this transformation process. Engage in self-care practices and nurture your body and mind. Exercise regularly, maintain a balanced diet, get sufficient rest, and participate in activities that bring joy and relaxation. A healthy and balanced lifestyle supports emotional resilience and aids in regaining trust.

Forgiving yourself and your ex-husband , is a significant milestone in rebuilding trust. Holding on to resentment and anger can impede the ability to trust others. Forgiveness is not a condonation of past actions, but a release of the emotional burden associated with them. It allows you to free yourself from the past and move forward with a lighter heart.

If you decide to enter a new romantic relationship, it's crucial to take things slowly. Rushing into new relationships can hinder the authentic development of trust. Invest time in getting to know your partner gradually, allowing trust to build naturally and authentically. Building a strong foundation takes patience and care. Incorporate positive self-affirmations into daily life. Remind yourself of your strengths and capacity for love and trust.

These affirmations counteract negative self-doubt and reinforce belief in your ability to trust again. Positive self-talk can be a powerful tool in regaining self-confidence.

Regaining trust after divorce is a multifaceted process that involves self-reflection, seeking professional guidance, open communication, setting realistic expectations, establishing boundaries, self-care, forgiveness, taking relationships slowly, and positive affirmations.

While the path may be challenging and marked with setbacks, it is possible to rebuild trust in yourself and others, leading to healthier and more fulfilling relationships in the future. Remember that healing is a journey, and it's perfectly acceptable to seek help and support along the way.

Affirmations of Peace

I am a beacon of light and love, radiating compassion and trust.

CHAPTER SIXTEEN

PAYING IT FORWARD

Consider using your triumphs as an opportunity to give back or support others who are going through similar challenges. Sharing your experiences and story can inspire and empower others on their journey. Offer mentorship or guidance to individuals facing divorce or other life challenges. Your wisdom and resilience can serve as a source of inspiration and support.

After emerging from the challenging and transformative journey of divorce, many individuals find themselves in a unique position to give back and support others who are navigating similar hardships. Paying it forward through mentorship can be a powerful and meaningful way to channel the lessons and experiences from divorce into a source of empowerment and support for others.

Mentorship after divorce goes beyond offering advice or guidance. It is a heartfelt commitment to providing understanding, empathy, and a helping hand to those who may be feeling lost, overwhelmed, or isolated in the aftermath of their own divorces. Here, we explore the significance and impact of mentorship after divorce and why it is valuable. Mentorship after divorce is rooted in the shared understanding of the emotional roller coaster that often accompanies the dissolution of marriage.

Those who have experienced divorce firsthand can relate to the feelings of grief, loss, anger, and confusion that can be overwhelming during this time. This shared empathy creates a unique bond between mentors and mentees, providing a safe space for individuals to express their emotions and share their experiences without judgment. When someone who has walked a similar path listens empathetically to the challenges faced by someone currently going through a divorce, it can offer a sense of validation and relief. Knowing they are not alone in their feelings and experiences can provide immense comfort and hope for those amid their divorce.

Mentorship provides an avenue for offering practical guidance and emotional support during and after divorce. Mentors can share insights on navigating divorce's legal, financial, and logistical aspects, driven by their own experiences and lessons learned. They can help mentees understand the importance of self-care, coping strategies for managing emotional distress, and techniques for maintaining a sense of balance in their lives. Mentors can serve as a source of encouragement, reminding mentees that healing is a process where recovery and personal growth are possible.

Through active listening, offering a compassionate ear, and sharing stories of resilience, mentors can instill hope and optimism in those who may be feeling overwhelmed by the challenges of divorce.

Divorce can often lead to feelings of isolation and loneliness. It may seem like no one understands the unique struggles and emotions that come with the end of a marriage. Mentorship after divorce creates a sense of community and belonging for both mentors and mentees. The mentors are connections that transcend individual experiences and build a support network.

For mentors, giving back by supporting others who are going through a similar journey can be profoundly fulfilling. It allows them to use their own experience to positively impact someone else's life. It reaffirms that their own struggles were not in vain but rather a source of wisdom and strength to be shared with others.

For mentees, knowing that there are people who genuinely care about their well-being and are willing to offer guidance and support can be a source of comfort and motivation. The sense of community created through mentorship can help combat the feelings of isolation that often accompany divorce.

One of the most profound impacts of mentorship after divorce is the potential to break the cycle of pain and hardship. By offering support and guidance to those in the early stages of divorce, mentors can help prevent their mentees from making the same mistakes or following in the same patterns that may have contributed to the breakdown of their own marriages.

Mentors can share insights into effective communication, conflict resolution, and personal growth that can empower their mentees to build healthier relationships in the future. They can encourage mentees to reflect on their own roles in their own marriages and take responsibility for their own actions, facilitating personal growth and self-awareness. By breaking the cycle, mentorship after divorce not only benefits the individuals directly involved but also has the potential to create healthier families and communities in the long run.

Paying it forward through mentorship after divorce is a profound and selfless act that can bring healing, hope, and positive change to the lives of those who have experienced the end of a marriage. It offers a powerful way to transform the pain and challenges of divorce into a source of strength, resilience, and empathy.

Through shared understanding, practical guidance, emotional support, a sense of community, and the potential to break the cycle of hardship, mentorship after divorce can have a profound and lasting impact on both the lives of both mentors and mentees.

Affirmations of Peace

I am a beacon of light and love, radiating compassion and empathy toward myself and others. My journey of soulful healing continues to unfold.

CHAPTER SEVENTEEN

THE END

Divorce, though an end to a marriage, is not the end of your journey. It's a catalyst for rebirth and provides opportunities to construct a life more aligned with your true self.

The first building block is vision. What does your ideal life look like? It's not just about big dreams and goals, but also the day-to-day reality you want to manifest. It could be pursuing a career change, returning to school, or dedicating more time to health and wellness. It could be relationships, community involvement, or personal development. Craft a vision that excites you and makes you look forward to the days ahead.

Focus on setting intentions. Unlike fleeting desires, intentions are deep-seated commitments to yourself and your future. They are the soul behind your goals, giving them purpose and direction. Set intentions that resonate with your core values and vision. They will act as your compass, guiding your decisions and actions as you navigate this new terrain.

With your vision and intentions in place, it's time to establish goals. Goals are the tangible milestones that mark your progress. They should be specific, measurable, achievable, relevant, and time-bound (SMART). But beyond the logistics of goal setting, it's important to connect emotionally with your goals.

They should feel meaningful and motivating, not just items on a checklist. As you lay these blocks, remember that building a new life is not a solo endeavor. Seek out community and support. This might include friends and family, divorce support groups, or professional help from pastors or therapists. These networks provide emotional support, practical advice, inspiration, and camaraderie. They remind you that you're not alone in this journey.

Action, vision, intention, and goals are crucial, but they are just the blueprint. Building a new life requires you to put those plans into action. This might involve stepping out of your comfort zone, facing fears, and embracing uncertainties.

It will require perseverance, resilience, and a willingness to adapt as you learn and grow. Taking a step forward, no matter how small, is a step toward the life you envision.

Throughout this book, we explored each of these building blocks in depth. Providing advice to help you construct a solid foundation for your future. From creating a vision board to setting and pursuing goals, from nurturing your support network.

You've been equipped with the tools and inspiration to build a life filled with happiness, purpose, and fulfillment.

After year 14, my divorce was final. There was nothing else to be written in this story; the relationship and marriage are over. I did not dwell on the what-ifs, because at the end of the movie, at the end of the story, at the end of the song, and at the end of the relationship, there's nothing else left. There's nothing else to be said. The chapter is over, and this book marks the end of a marriage that lasted for 14 years.

Blessings to each and every person who has purchased and read the words in my book Piecing Back the Peace. I pray that it has been a blessing to you. I pray that if any young ladies or young wives are struggling in a relationship and need God to free them, I hope that the words that I've shared with you have been an inspiration.

I hope that you gained encouragement, I hope that you have strength that you didn't have before, but more importantly, I pray that God grant you peace in your relationships, in your finances, in your spirituality, in your family, in your home, and in love.

Sincerely, Dr. Tammy Cannon Williams

Affirmations of Peace

Now that we have reached the end, please remind yourself not to dwell on the what-ifs and the possibilities of what could have happened. The end is just that – THE END.

Questions to Consider

1. What were the initial feelings you experienced after your divorce, and have they evolved?

2. How do you define your sense of self, independent of your past relationship?

3. What are the most significant lessons you've learned about yourself through the divorce?

4. In what ways have you practiced self-compassion during your healing process?

5. How have your perspectives on love, relationships, and marriage changed?

6. What steps have you taken to create a supportive and nurturing environment for yourself?

7. How do you handle feelings of loneliness or sadness when they arise?

8. What are your personal boundaries, and how do you assert them in relationships and other areas of your life?

9. How do you prioritize your well-being and happiness daily?

10. What are your goals for the future, and how do they reflect your true desires and values?

11. How have you rebuilt or strengthened your sense of independence since your divorce?

12. In what ways have you engaged with your community or sought out new supportive networks?

13. What new hobbies or interests have you explored as part of your journey to rediscovery?

14. How do you approach dating or new relationships after your experience with divorce?

15. What are the biggest fears you've overcome, and how did you manage to do so?

16. How do you maintain a positive outlook when facing setbacks or challenges?

17. What strategies do you use to manage stress and maintain mental and emotional health?

18. How do you celebrate your achievements and milestones, no matter how small?

19. How do you continue to grow and learn as an individual?

20. Looking back from where you started to where you are now, what are you most proud of achieving or changing in your life?

About the Author

Dr. Tammy Cannon Williams is a remarkable author, speaker, and advocate who has overcome adversity with unwavering resilience and grace. As a divorced mother of three children, she faced the daunting task of rebuilding her life after divorce, and her journey from heartbreak to healing has inspired countless individuals on their paths to recovery.

Tammy's story is a testament to the strength of the human spirit. She navigated the challenges of divorce with determination, embracing the opportunity for self-discovery and personal growth. Through her experiences, she learned the power of resilience, the importance of self-care, and the transformative nature of self-compassion.

Her candid and heartfelt writing draws from her own life experiences, offering solace and guidance to those who have traveled a similar road. Tammy's words resonate with authenticity and empathy, providing hope for those seeking to rebuild their lives after their divorce.

In addition to her role as an author, Tammy is a dedicated mother who cherishes her three children and the lessons they've taught her about love, strength, and the enduring bond of family.

She is now happily married, a testament to her belief in the possibility of finding love and happiness even after the most challenging of life's trials.

Tammy's journey is a source of inspiration for all who have faced adversity and sought to emerge stronger, wiser, and more resilient on the other side. Her story serves as a reminder that, with courage and determination, we cannot only survive life's challenges but thrive and find fulfillment in the process.

Author Info.

Website: drtammycannon.com
IG: dr.tammy_70
Email: info@drtammycannon.com

Publisher Info.

Russell E Ivory III

- WatchMeGrowTheMovement (Instagram)
- WatchMeGrowTheMovement (TikTok)
- GusePublishing@gmail
- RussellIvory (YouTube)

Made in the USA
Columbia, SC
30 May 2024

6da3854e-b11f-4f10-9f17-0f9103f07e84R02